GW00339195

Keto Air Fryer and Keto Chaffle 2021

The perfect guide to start weight loss with ketogenic diet in less 2 week

Lisa McAllister

© Copyright 2021 by **Lisa McAllister**- All rights reserved.

The following Book is reproduced below with the goal of providing information that is as accurate and reliable as possible. Regardless, purchasing this Book can be seen as consent to the fact that both the publisher and the author of this book are in no way experts on the topics discussed within and that any recommendations or suggestions that are made herein are for entertainment purposes only. Professionals should be consulted as needed prior to undertaking any of the action endorsed herein.

This declaration is deemed fair and valid by both the American Bar Association and the Committee of Publishers Association and is legally binding throughout the United States.

Furthermore, the transmission, duplication, or reproduction of any of the following work including specific information will be considered an illegal act irrespective of if it is done electronically or in print. This extends to creating a secondary or tertiary copy of the work or a recorded copy and is only allowed with the express written consent from the Publisher. All additional right reserved.

The information in the following pages is broadly considered a truthful and accurate account of facts and as such, any inattention, use, or misuse of the information in question by the reader will render any resulting actions solely under their purview. There are no scenarios in which the publisher or the original author of this work can be in any fashion deemed liable for any hardship or damages that may befall them after undertaking information described herein.

Additionally, the information in the following pages is intended only for informational purposes and should thus be thought of as universal. As befitting its nature, it is presented without assurance regarding its prolonged validity or interim quality. Trademarks that are mentioned are done without written consent and can in no way be considered an endorsement from the trademark holder.

Contents

Introduction

Life gets busy, especially when you have children, meetings, and other obligations.

Too often healthy eating falls low on the priority list, and people default to processed convenience foods laden with sugar and carbs.

Is very important curb mealtime stress by combining low-carb, keto-friendly recipes with America's latest kitchen trend: everything with the air fryer.

Air fryers have become extremely popular in the last few years due to their ease of use, their speed, and the healthier foods they produce.

Tired of waiting for your oven to heat up (not to mention your house, especially in summer)?

What about soggy leftovers after reheating in the microwave?

The air fryer has you covered! Almost any deep-fried or oven-baked dish can be made in an air fryer. Preparing your favorite keto dishes in record time with little cleanup has never been easier.

This guide gives you her best tips and tricks for success on the keto diet and offers up a wide variety of delicious dishes, from air fryer classics like onion rings and chicken wings to unexpected additions like cookies and even omelets.

Keto Air Fryer will help you make quick and delicious meals, save time in the kitchen, and enjoy the family!

We hope you will benefit from this book and use the recipes we have prepared for you on a daily basis.

Also in this book you will find keto chaffle recipes, the new craze that has hit everyone.

So whether you crave sweet or savoury you can satisfy your taste buds with this bonus we have reserved at the end of this book.

Are you ready to get started?

Breakfast recipes

Golden Egg Bagels

Preparation Time: 4 minutes
Cooking Time: 16 minutes
Servings: 8

Ingredients:

- 2 eggs
- 4 tsp. dry yeast
- 4-5 cups all-purpose flour
- 1 tbsp. canola oil and kosher salt
- 1-1/2 tbsp. sugar

Directions

1. Whisk eggs, sugar, yeast, lukewarm, water, and oil. Add flour and salt to prepare the dough.
2. Make a long rope with the dough, locking both ends.
3. Preheat the Air Fryer Grill to 2000C or 4000F.
4. Boil bagels in sugar and salt for 45 seconds.
5. Drain bagels, brush with egg white and bake for 15-20 mins.

Nutrition: Calories: 164 Protein: 6.6g Fat: 2.1g.

Wild Blueberry Bagels

Preparation Time: 11 minutes
Cooking Time: 5 minutes
Servings: 1

Ingredients:

- 1 bagel
- 1 tbsp. low-fat cream cheese
- 2 tbsp. frozen wild blueberries
- 1/4 tsp. cinnamon

Directions

1. Preheat the Air Fryer Grill to 1900C or 3750F
2. Toast the bagel for 3-5 minutes.
3. Spread cream cheese; add blueberry toppings, and cinnamon.

Nutrition: Calories: 155 Protein: 6g Fat: 3.5g

Southwestern Waffles

Preparation Time: 8 minutes
Cooking Time: 6 minutes
Servings: 4

Ingredients:

- 1 egg, fried
- 1/4 avocado, chopped
- 1 frozen waffle
- 1 tbsp. salsa

Directions

1. Preheat the Air Fryer Grill to 2000C or 4000F.
2. Bake the waffles for 5-7 minutes.
3. Add avocado, fried eggs and fresh salsa as toppings.

Nutrition: Calories: 207 Protein: 9g Fat: 12g

Pumpkin Spice Bagels

Preparation Time: 18 minutes
Cooking Time: 12 minutes
Servings: 2

Ingredients:

- 1 egg
- 1 cup flour
- 1/2 tsp. pumpkin spice
- 1/2 cup Greek yogurt

Directions

1. Create a dough with flour, pie spice, yogurt, and pumpkin in a stand mixer.
2. Shape the dough into a few ropes and make bagels.
3. Apply egg and water mixture over the bagels.
4. Preheat the Air Fryer Grill to 1900C or 3750F and bake for 20-25 minutes.

Nutrition: Calories: 183 Protein: 9.4g Fat: 2g.

Bacon, Egg and Cheese Breakfast Hash

Preparation Time: 12 minutes
Cooking Time: 35 minutes
Servings: 4

Ingredients:

- 2 slices of bacon
- 4 tiny potatoes
- 1/4 tomato
- 1 egg
- 1/4 cup of shredded cheese

Direction

1. Preheat the Air Fryer Grill to 2000C or 4000F on bake mode. Set bits of bacon on a double-layer tin foil.
2. Cut the vegetables to put over the bacon. Crack an egg over it.
3. Shape the tin foil into a bowl and cook it in the Air Fryer Grill at 1770C or 3500F for 15-20 minutes. Put some shredded cheese on top.

Nutrition: Calories: 150.5 Protein: 6g Fat: 6g.

Southwestern Hash with Eggs

Preparation Time: 25 minutes
Cooking Time: 45 minutes
Servings: 4

Ingredients:

- 1-1/2 lbs. pork steak
- 1 tsp. vegetable oil
- 1 large potato, peeled and cubed
- 1 medium-sized onion, chopped
- 1 garlic clove, minced
- 1/2 cup green pepper, chopped
- 1 can diced tomatoes and green chilies
- 1 beef bouillon cube
- 1/2 tsp. ground cumin
- 1/2 tsp. salt
- 1/4 tsp. pepper
- 1/8 tsp. cayenne pepper
- 4 eggs
- 3/4 cup shredded cheddar cheese
- 4 corn tortillas (six inches)

Directions

1. Cook pork in oil until brown and add potato, onion, garlic, green pepper. Cook for 4 minutes.
2. Stir in tomatoes, bouillon, cumin, salt, pepper, and cayenne. Cook with low heat until potatoes become tender.

3. Create four wells inside the hash and crack eggs into them.
4. Bake it in the Air Fryer Grill uncovered for 10-12 minutes at 1770C or 3500F and scatter some cheese over it.
5. Serve over tortillas.

Nutrition: Calories: 520 Protein: 49g Fat: 23g

Poultry recipes

Chicken Rochambeau with Mushroom Sauce

Preparation time: 25 minutes
Cooking time: 30 minutes
Serving: 4

Ingredients

- 1 tablespoon melted butter
- ¼ cup all-purpose flour
- 4 chicken tenders, cut in half crosswise
- 4 slices ham, ¼-inch thick, large enough to cover an English muffin
- 2 English muffins split in halves
- Salt and ground black pepper, to taste
- Cooking spray

Mushroom Sauce:

- 2 tablespoons butter
- ½ cup chopped mushrooms
- ½ cup chopped green onions
- 2 tablespoons flour
- 1 cup chicken broth
- 1½ teaspoons Worcestershire sauce
- ¼ teaspoon garlic powder

Direction

1. Put the butter in a baking pan. Mix the flour, salt, and ground black pepper in a shallow dish. Roll the chicken tenders over to coat well.

2. Arrange the chicken in the baking pan and flip to coat with the melted butter.
3. Slide the pan into the air fryer oven. Press the Power Button. Cook at 390°F (199°C) for 10 minutes.
4. Flip the tenders halfway through.
5. When cooking is complete, the juices of chicken tenders should run clear.
6. Meanwhile, make the mushroom sauce: melt 2 tablespoons of butter in a saucepan over medium-high heat.
7. Stir in the mushrooms and onions to the saucepan and sauté for 3 minutes or until the onions are translucent.
8. Gently mix in the flour, broth, Worcestershire sauce, and garlic powder until smooth.
9. Reduce the heat to low and simmer for 5 minutes or until it has a thick consistency. Keep the sauce aside until ready to serve.
10. When cooking is complete, remove the baking pan from the air fryer oven and set the ham slices into the air flow racks.
11. Cook for 5 minutes. Flip the ham slices halfway through.
12. When cooking is complete, the ham slices should be heated through.
13. Remove the ham slices from the air fryer oven and set in the English muffin halves and warm for 1 minute.
14. Spread each ham slice on top of each muffin half, then place each chicken tender over the ham slice.
15. Transfer to the air fryer oven for 2 minutes.
16. Serve with the sauce on top.

Nutrition: Calories: 175 Protein: 12g Fat: 6.7g

Chicken Schnitzel

Preparation time: 15 minutes
Cooking time: 5 minutes
Serving: 4

Ingredient

- ½ cup all-purpose flour
- 1 teaspoon marjoram
- ½ teaspoon thyme
- 1 teaspoon dried parsley flakes
- ½ teaspoon salt
- 1 egg
- 1 teaspoon lemon juice
- 1 teaspoon water
- 1 cup breadcrumbs
- 4 chicken tenders, pounded thin, cut in half lengthwise
- Cooking spray

Direction

1. Spritz the air flow racks with cooking spray.
2. Combine the flour, marjoram, thyme, parsley, and salt in a shallow dish. Stir to mix well.
3. Whisk the egg with lemon juice and water in a large bowl. Pour the breadcrumbs in a separate shallow dish.

4. Roll the chicken halves in the flour mixture first, then in the egg mixture, and then roll over the breadcrumbs to coat well. Shake the excess off.
5. Arrange the chicken halves in the air flow racks and spritz with cooking spray on both sides.
6. Slide the racks into the air fryer oven. Press the Power Button. Cook at 390°F (199°C) for 5 minutes.
7. Flip the halves halfway through.
8. When cooking is complete, the chicken halves should be golden brown and crispy.
9. Serve immediately.

Nutrition: Calories: 133 Protein: 19g Fat: 12g

Chicken Shawarma

Preparation time: 10 minutes
Cooking time: 18 minutes
Serving: 4
Ingredient

- 1½ lb. (680 g) chicken thighs
- 1¼ teaspoon kosher salt, divided
- 2 tablespoons plus 1 teaspoon olive oil, divided
- 2/3 cup plus 2 tablespoons plain Greek yogurt, divided
- 2 tablespoons freshly squeezed lemon juice (about 1 medium lemon)
- 4 garlic cloves, minced, divided
- 1 tablespoon Shawarma Seasoning
- 4 pita breads, cut in half
- 2 cups cherry tomatoes
- ½ small cucumber, peeled, deseeded, and chopped
- 1 tablespoon chopped fresh parsley

Direction

1. Season the chicken thighs on both sides with 1 teaspoon of kosher salt. Place in a resealable plastic bag and set aside while you make the marinade.

2. In a small bowl, mix 2 tablespoons of olive oil, 2 tablespoons of yogurt, the lemon juice, 3 garlic cloves, and Shawarma Seasoning until thoroughly combined. Pour the marinade over the chicken. Wrap the bag, squeezing out as much air as possible. And massage the chicken to coat it with the sauce. Set aside.

3. Wrap 2 pita breads each in two pieces of aluminum foil and place on a baking pan.
4. Slide the pan into the air fryer oven. Press the Power Button. Cook at 300°F (150°C) for 6 minutes.
5. After 3 minutes, remove from the air fryer oven and turn over the foil packets. Return to the air fryer oven and continue cooking. When cooking is complete, remove from the air fryer oven and place the foil-wrapped pitas on the top of the air fryer oven to keep warm.
6. Pull out the chicken from the marinade, letting the excess drip off into the bag. Place them on the baking pan. Arrange the tomatoes around the sides of the chicken. Discard the marinade.
7. Slide the pan into the air fryer oven. Cook for 12 minutes.
8. After 6 minutes, remove from the air fryer oven and turn over the chicken. Return to the air fryer oven and continue cooking.
9. Wrap the cucumber in a paper towel to remove as much moisture as possible. Place them in a small bowl. Add the remaining yogurt, kosher salt, olive oil, garlic clove, and parsley. Whisk until combined.
10. Pull out the pan from the air fryer oven and place the chicken on a cutting board. Cut each thigh into several pieces. Unwrap the pitas. Spread a tablespoon of sauce into a pita half. Add some chicken and add 2 roasted tomatoes. Serve.

Nutrition: Calories: 199 Protein: 22g Fat: 6g

Chicken Skewers with Corn Salad

Preparation time: 17 minutes
Cooking time: 10 minutes
Serving: 4

Ingredient

- 1 lb. (454 g) chicken breast, cut into 1½-inch chunks
- 1 green bell pepper, deseeded and cut into 1-inch pieces
- 1 red bell pepper, deseeded and cut into 1-inch pieces
- 1 large onion, cut into large chunks
- 2 tablespoons fajita seasoning
- 3 tablespoons vegetable oil, divided
- 2 teaspoons kosher salt, divided
- 2 cups corn, drained
- ¼ teaspoon granulated garlic
- 1 teaspoon freshly squeezed lime juice
- 1 tablespoon mayonnaise
- 3 tablespoons grated Parmesan cheese

Direction

1. Situate the chicken, bell peppers, and onion in a large bowl. Add the fajita seasoning, 2 tablespoons of vegetable oil, and 1½ teaspoons of kosher salt. Toss to coat evenly.
2. Alternate the chicken and vegetables on the skewers, making about 12 skewers.

3. Place the corn in a medium bowl and add the remaining vegetable oil. Add the remaining kosher salt and the garlic, and toss to coat. Place the corn in an even layer on a baking pan and place the skewers on top.
4. Slide the pan into the air fryer oven. Press the Power Button. Cook at 375°F (190°C) for 10 minutes.
5. After about 5 minutes, remove from the air fryer oven and turn the skewers. Return to the air fryer oven and continue cooking.
6. When cooking is complete, remove from the air fryer oven. Place the skewers on a platter. Put the corn back to the bowl and combine with the lime juice, mayonnaise, and Parmesan cheese. Stir to mix well. Serve the skewers with the corn.

Nutrition: Calories: 166 Protein: 17g Fat: 11g

Chicken Thighs in Waffles

Preparation time: 1 hour 20 minutes
Cooking time: 20 minutes
Serving: 4
Ingredient
For the chicken:

- 4 chicken thighs, skin on
- 1 cup low-fat buttermilk
- ½ cup all-purpose flour
- ½ teaspoon garlic powder
- ½ teaspoon mustard powder
- 1 teaspoon kosher salt
- ½ teaspoon freshly ground black pepper
- ¼ cup honey, for serving
- Cooking spray

For the waffles:

- ½ cup all-purpose flour
- ½ cup whole wheat pastry flour
- 1 large egg, beaten
- 1 cup low-fat buttermilk
- 1 teaspoon baking powder
- 2 tablespoons canola oil
- ½ teaspoon kosher salt
- 1 tablespoon granulated sugar

Direction

1. Combine the chicken thighs with buttermilk in a large bowl. Wrap the bowl in plastic and refrigerate to marinate for at least an hour.

2. Spritz the air flow racks with cooking spray. Combine the flour, mustard powder, garlic powder, salt, and black pepper in a shallow dish. Stir to mix well.

3. Remove the thighs from the buttermilk and pat dry with paper towels. Sit the bowl of buttermilk aside.

4. Dip the thighs in the flour mixture first, then into the buttermilk, and then into the flour mixture. Shake the excess off. Arrange the thighs in the air flow racks and spritz with cooking spray.

5. Slide the racks into the air fryer oven. Press the Power Button. Cook at 360°F (182°C) for 20 minutes. Flip the thighs halfway through. When cooking is complete, an instant-read thermometer inserted in the thickest part of the chicken thighs should register at least 165°F (74°C).

6. Meanwhile, make the waffles: combine the ingredients for the waffles in a large bowl. Stir to mix well, then arrange the mixture in a waffle iron and cook until a golden and fragrant waffle forms.

7. Remove the waffles from the waffle iron and slice into 4 pieces. Remove the chicken thighs from the air fryer oven and allow to cool for 5 minutes.

8. Arrange each chicken thigh on each waffle piece and drizzle with 1 tablespoon of honey. Serve warm.

Nutrition: Calories: 188 Protein: 21g Fat: 9g

Chicken Thighs with Radish Slaw

Preparation time: 10 minutes
Cooking time: 27 minutes
Serving: 4

Ingredient

- 4 bone-in, skin-on chicken thighs
- 1½ teaspoon kosher salt, divided
- 1 tablespoon smoked paprika
- ½ teaspoon granulated garlic
- ½ teaspoon dried oregano
- ¼ teaspoon freshly ground black pepper
- 3 cups shredded cabbage
- ½ small red onion, thinly sliced
- 4 large radishes, julienned
- 3 tablespoons red wine vinegar
- 2 tablespoons olive oil
- Cooking spray

Direction

1. Sprinkle the salt in the chicken thighs on both sides with 1 teaspoon of kosher salt. In a small bowl, combine the paprika, garlic, oregano, and black pepper. Sprinkle half this mixture over the skin sides of the thighs. Spritz a baking pan with cooking spray and place the thighs skin-side down on the pan. Sprinkle the remaining spice mixture over the other sides of the chicken pieces.

2. Slide the pan into the air fryer oven. Press the Power Button. Cook at 375°F (190°C) for 27 minutes.

3. After 10 minutes, remove from the air fryer oven and turn over the chicken thighs. Return to the air fryer oven and continue cooking.

4. While the chicken cooks, place the cabbage, onion, and radishes in a large bowl. Sprinkle with the remaining kosher salt, vinegar, and olive oil. Toss to coat.

5. After another 9 to 10 minutes, remove from the air fryer oven and place the chicken thighs on a cutting board. Place the cabbage mixture in the pan and toss with the chicken fat and spices.

6. Arrange the cabbage in an even layer on the pan and place the chicken on it, skin-side up. Return to the air fryer oven and continue cooking. Roast for another 7 to 8 minutes.

7. When cooking is complete, the cabbage is just becoming tender. Remove from the air fryer oven. Taste and adjust the seasoning if necessary. Serve.

Nutrition: Calories: 187 Protein: 21g Fat: 11g

Chicken with Asparagus, Beans, and Arugula

Preparation time: 20 minutes
Cooking time: 25 minutes

Serving: 2

Ingredient

- 1 cup canned cannellini beans, rinsed
- 1½ tablespoons red wine vinegar
- 1 garlic clove, minced
- 2 tablespoons extra-virgin olive oil, divided
- Salt and ground black pepper, to taste
- ½ red onion, sliced thinly
- 8 ounces (227 g) asparagus, trimmed and cut into 1-inch lengths
- 2 (8-ounce / 227-g) boneless, skinless chicken breasts, trimmed
- ¼ teaspoon paprika
- ½ teaspoon ground coriander
- 2 ounces (57 g) baby arugula, rinsed and drained

Direction

1. Warm the beans in microwave for 1 minute and combine with red wine vinegar, garlic, 1 tablespoon of olive oil, ¼ teaspoon of salt, and ¼ teaspoon of ground black pepper in a bowl. Stir to mix well.
2. Combine the onion with 1/8 teaspoon of salt, 1/8 teaspoon of ground black pepper, and 2 teaspoons of olive oil in a separate bowl. Toss to coat well.
3. Place the onion in the air flow racks.
4. Slide the racks into the air fryer oven. Press the Power Button. Cook at 400°F (205°C) for 2 minutes.
5. After 2 minutes, add the asparagus for 8 minutes. Stir the vegetable halfway through.

6. When cooking is complete, the asparagus should be tender.
7. Transfer the onion and asparagus to the bowl with beans. Set aside.
8. Toss the chicken breasts with remaining ingredients, except for the baby arugula, in a large bowl.
9. Put the chicken breasts in the air flow racks. Slide the racks into the air fryer oven. Cook for 14 minutes. Flip the breasts halfway through.
10. When cooking is complete, the internal temperature of the chicken reaches at least 165°F (74°C).
11. Remove the chicken from the air fryer oven and serve on an aluminum foil with asparagus, beans, onion, and arugula. Sprinkle with salt and ground black pepper. Toss to serve.

Nutrition: Calories: 166 Protein: 19g Fat: 9g

Chicken with Potatoes and Corn

Preparation time: 10 minutes
Cooking time: 25 minutes
Serving: 4

Ingredient

- 4 bone-in, skin-on chicken thighs
- 2 teaspoons kosher salt, divided
- 1 cup Bisquick baking mix
- ½ cup butter, melted, divided
- 1 pound (454 g) small red potatoes, quartered
- 3 ears corn, shucked and cut into rounds 1- to 1½-inches thick
- 1/3 cup heavy whipping cream
- ½ teaspoon freshly ground black pepper

Direction

1. Season the chicken on all sides with 1 teaspoon of kosher salt. Place the baking mix in a shallow dish. Brush the thighs on all sides with ¼ cup of butter, then dredge them in the baking mix, coating them all on sides. Place the chicken in the center of a baking pan.

2. Situate the potatoes in a large bowl with 2 tablespoons of butter and toss to coat. Place them on one side of the chicken on the pan.

3. Place the corn in a medium bowl and drizzle with the remaining butter. Sprinkle with ¼ teaspoon of kosher salt and toss to coat. Place on the pan on the other side of the chicken.

4. Slide the pan into the air fryer oven. Press the Power Button. Cook at 375°F (190°C) for 25 minutes.

5. After 20 minutes, remove from the air fryer oven and transfer the potatoes back to the bowl. Return the pan to air fryer oven and continue cooking.

6. As the chicken continues cooking, add the cream, black pepper, and remaining kosher salt to the potatoes. Lightly crush the potatoes with a potato masher.

7. When cooking is complete, the corn should be tender and the chicken cooked through, reading 165°F (74°C) on a meat thermometer. Pull out the pan from the air fryer oven and serve the chicken with the smashed potatoes and corn on the side.

Nutrition: Calories: 199 Protein: 24g Fat: 6g

Beef recipes

Salsa Beef Meatballs

Preparation time: 10 minutes
Cooking time: 10 minutes
Serving: 4

Ingredient

- 1-pound (454 g) ground beef (85% lean)
- ½ cup salsa
- ¼ cup diced green or red bell peppers
- 1 large egg, beaten
- ¼ cup chopped onions
- ½ teaspoon chili powder
- 1 clove garlic, minced
- ½ teaspoon ground cumin
- 1 teaspoon fine sea salt
- Lime wedges, for serving
- Cooking spray

Direction

1. Spritz the air fry basket with cooking spray.
2. Combine all the ingredients in a large bowl. Stir to mix well.
3. Divide and shape the mixture into 1-inch balls. Arrange the balls in the basket and spritz with cooking spray.
4. Select Air Fry, Super Convection. Set temperature to 350°F (180°C) and set time to 10 minutes. Press Start/Stop to begin preheating.

5. Once preheated, place the basket on the air fry position. Flip the balls with tongs halfway through.
6. When cooking is complete, the balls should be well browned.
7. Transfer the balls on a plate and squeeze the lime wedges over before serving.

Nutrition: Calories: 348 Fat: 19g Protein: 46g

Simple Ground Beef with Zucchini

Preparation time: 5 minutes
Cooking time: 12 minutes
Serving: 4

Ingredient

- 1½ pounds (680 g) ground beef
- 1 pound (454 g) chopped zucchini
- 2 tablespoons extra-virgin olive oil
- 1 teaspoon dried oregano
- 1 teaspoon dried basil
- 1 teaspoon dried rosemary
- 2 tablespoons fresh chives, chopped

Direction

1. In a large bowl, combine all the ingredients, except for the chives, until well blended.
2. Place the beef and zucchini mixture in the baking pan.
3. Select Bake, Super Convection, set temperature to 400°F (205°C) and set time to 12 minutes. Press Start/Stop to begin preheating.
4. Once preheated, place the pan on the bake position.
5. When cooking is complete, the beef should be browned and the zucchini should be tender.
6. Divide the beef and zucchini mixture among four serving dishes. Top with fresh chives and serve hot.

Nutrition: Calories: 311 Fat: 20g Protein: 41g

Sumptuous Beef and Pork Sausage Meatloaf

Preparation time: 10 minutes
Cooking time: 25 minutes
Serving: 4

Ingredient

- ¾ pound (340 g) ground chuck
- 4 ounces (113 g) ground pork sausage
- 2 eggs, beaten
- 1 cup Parmesan cheese, grated
- 1 cup chopped shallot
- 3 tablespoons plain milk
- 1 tablespoon oyster sauce
- 1 tablespoon fresh parsley
- 1 teaspoon garlic paste
- 1 teaspoon chopped porcini mushrooms
- ½ teaspoon cumin powder
- Seasoned salt and crushed red pepper flakes, to taste

Direction

1. In a large bowl, combine all the ingredients until well blended.
2. Place the meat mixture in the baking pan. Use a spatula to press the mixture to fill the pan.

3. Select Bake, Super Convection, set temperature to 360°F (182°C) and set time to 25 minutes. Press Start/Stop to begin preheating.

4. Once preheated, place the pan on the bake position.

5. When cooking is complete, the meatloaf should be well browned.

6. Let the meatloaf rest for 5 minutes. Transfer to a serving dish and slice. Serve warm.

Nutrition: Calories: 317 Fat: 23g Protein: 46g

Lahmacun (Turkish Pizza)

Preparation time: 20 minutes
Cooking time: 10 minutes
Serving: 4

Ingredient

- 4 (6-inch) flour tortillas

For the Meat Topping:

- 4 ounces (113 g) ground lamb or 85% lean ground beef
- ¼ cup finely chopped green bell pepper
- ¼ cup chopped fresh parsley
- 1 small plum tomato, deseeded and chopped
- 2 tablespoons chopped yellow onion
- 1 garlic clove, minced
- 2 teaspoons tomato paste
- ¼ teaspoon sweet paprika
- ¼ teaspoon ground cumin
- ¼ teaspoon red pepper flakes
- 1/8 teaspoon ground allspice
- 1/8 teaspoon kosher salt
- 1/8 teaspoon black pepper

For Serving:

- ¼ cup chopped fresh mint
- 1 teaspoon extra-virgin olive oil
- 1 lemon, cut into wedges

Direction

1. Combine all the ingredients for the meat topping in a medium bowl until well mixed.
2. Lay the tortillas on a clean work surface. Spoon the meat mixture on the tortillas and spread all over.
3. Place the tortillas in the air fry basket.
4. Select Air Fry, Super Convection. Set temperature to 400°F (205°C) and set time to 10 minutes. Press Start/Stop to begin preheating.
5. Once preheated, place the basket on the air fry position.
6. When cooking is complete, the edge of the tortilla should be golden and the meat should be lightly browned.
7. Transfer them to a serving dish. Top with chopped fresh mint and drizzle with olive oil. Squeeze the lemon wedges on top and serve.

Nutrition: Calories: 313 Fat: 27g Protein: 31g

Thai Curry Beef Meatballs

Preparation time: 5 minutes
Cooking time: 15 minutes
Serving: 4
Ingredient

- 1-pound (454 g) ground beef
- 1 tablespoon sesame oil
- 2 teaspoons chopped lemongrass
- 1 teaspoon red Thai curry paste
- 1 teaspoon Thai seasoning blend
- Juice and zest of ½ lime
- Cooking spray

Direction

1. Spritz the air fry basket with cooking spray.
2. In a medium bowl, combine all the ingredients until well blended.
3. Shape the meat mixture into 24 meatballs and arrange them in the basket.
4. Select Air Fry, Super Convection. Set temperature to 380°F (193°C) and set time to 15 minutes. Press Start/Stop to begin preheating.
5. Once preheated, place the basket on the air fry position. Flip the meatballs halfway through.
6. When cooking is complete, the meatballs should be browned.
7. Transfer the meatballs to plates. Let cool for 5 minutes before serving.

Nutrition: Calories: 338 Fat: 29g Protein: 56g

Stuffed Beef Tenderloin with Feta Cheese

Preparation time: 10 minutes
Cooking time: 10 minutes
Serving: 4

Ingredient

- 1½ pounds (680 g) beef tenderloin, pounded to ¼ inch thick
- 3 teaspoons sea salt
- 1 teaspoon ground black pepper
- 2 ounces (57 g) creamy goat cheese
- ½ cup crumbled feta cheese
- ¼ cup finely chopped onions
- 2 cloves garlic, minced
- Cooking spray

Direction

1. Spritz the air fry basket with cooking spray.
2. Unfold the beef tenderloin on a clean work surface. Rub the salt and pepper all over the beef tenderloin to season.
3. Make the filling for the stuffed beef tenderloins: Combine the goat cheese, feta, onions, and garlic in a medium bowl. Stir until well blended.

4. Spoon the mixture in the center of the tenderloin. Roll the tenderloin up tightly like rolling a burrito and use some kitchen twine to tie the tenderloin.
5. Arrange the tenderloin in the air fry basket.
6. Select Air Fry, Super Convection. Set temperature to 400°F (205°C) and set time to 10 minutes. Press Start/Stop to begin preheating.
7. Once preheated, place the basket on the air fry position. Flip the tenderloin halfway through.
8. When cooking is complete, the instant-read thermometer inserted in the center of the tenderloin should register 135°F (57°C) for medium-rare.
9. Transfer to a platter and serve immediately.

Nutrition: Calories: 321 Fat: 11g Protein: 30g

Teriyaki Beef Short Ribs with Pomegranate

Preparation time: 15 minutes
Cooking time: 1 hour
Serving: 4 to 6

Ingredient

- 1 cup tamari soy sauce or dark soy sauce
- ½ cup packed brown sugar
- ¼ cup pomegranate molasses
- 2 or 3 scallions, finely chopped (both white and green parts)
- 4 cloves garlic, minced
- 1 tablespoon oyster sauce
- 2 teaspoons Worcestershire sauce
- 2 teaspoons mirin
- 1 teaspoon vegetable oil
- 1 teaspoon grated fresh ginger
- 1 teaspoon Asian chili sauce
- 6 beef short ribs, 3½ to 4 inches long and 2 inches thick
- Chopped scallion, for garnish
- 1/3 cup pomegranate seeds, for garnish

Direction

1. Combine the marinade ingredients in a saucepan and simmer over medium heat for 3 to 5 minutes, until the sugar has dissolved, stirring occasionally. Remove from the heat and let the mixture cool for 30 minutes. Divide the marinade into two

equal portions. Store one half in the refrigerator for basting. Use the remaining half as the marinade.

2. Trim off any excess fat or straggling meat from the surface of the ribs. Do not attempt to remove any internal fat. Place the ribs in a resealable plastic bag and add the marinade. Using tongs, gently turn the ribs to coat. Seal the bag and place in the refrigerator for 6 to 12 hours.

3. Prepare the grill for medium heat with indirect cooking.

4. Set a tumble basket on a large cutting board. This will keep your floors and countertop clean. Remove the ribs from the bag and place them in the basket. Discard any marinade left in the bag. Secure the basket.

5. Place the basket on the preheated grill with a drip pan underneath, making sure that it doesn't get in the way of the basket as it turns. Cook for 1 to 1½ hours, or until the ribs have rendered the majority of their fat and have reached an internal temperature of 170°F (77°C) to 180°F (82°C).

6. Heat the reserved marinade in a bowl in the microwave for 1 minute. Stir. Begin basting with this mixture during the last 20 to 30 minutes of cooking time.

7. Remove the basket from the grill and place on a heat-resistant cutting board. Let the ribs rest for 5 minutes or so. Carefully open the basket and plate the ribs. Serve garnished with the chopped scallion and pomegranate seeds.

Nutrition: Calories: 333 Fat: 23g Protein: 32g

Prime Beef Rib Roast

Preparation time: 10 minutes
Cooking time: 2 hours
Serving: 2

Ingredient

- 1 (12 pound / 5.4-kg) bone-in beef rib roast (a four-bone roast)
- 3 tablespoons kosher salt
- 1 ½ tablespoons fresh ground black pepper
- Horseradish sauce
- ½ cup sour cream
- ¼ cup prepared horseradish
- 2 tablespoons Dijon mustard
- Fist sized chunk of smoking wood (or 1 cup wood chips)

Direction

1. Season the rib roast with the salt and pepper. Refrigerate for at least two hours, preferably overnight.
2. One hour before cooking, remove the rib roast from the refrigerator. Truss the roast, then skewer it on the rotisserie spit, securing it with the spit forks. Let the beef rest at room temperature until the grill is pre-heated. Submerge the smoking wood in water and let it soak until the grill is ready.
3. Set the grill up for indirect medium-high heat with the drip pan in the middle of the grill.

4. Put the spit on the grill, start the motor spinning, and make sure the drip pan is centered beneath the rib roast. Add the smoking wood to the fire, close the lid, and cook the beef until it reaches 120°F (49°C) in its thickest part for medium-rare, about 2 hours. (Cook to 115°F (46°C) for rare, 130°F (54°C) for medium.)

5. Remove the rib roast from the rotisserie spit and remove the twine trussing the roast. Be careful - the spit and forks are blazing hot. Let the beef rest for 15 minutes, and while the beef is resting, whisk together the ingredients for the horseradish sauce. To carve the beef, cut the bones off of the roast, then slice the roast and serve.

Nutrition: Calories: 368 Fat: 16g Protein: 26g

Steak with Olive Tapenade

Preparation Time: 11 minutes
Cooking Time: 22 minutes
Serving: 4
Ingredients:
Steak

- 1-1/4 lb. sirloin steak
- 1 tablespoon olive oil
- Salt and pepper to taste

Tapenade

- 1/2 cup red onion, chopped
- 1 clove garlic, minced
- 1 green bell pepper, chopped
- 1 tablespoon fresh parsley, chopped
- 2 tablespoons capers
- 1 cup Kalamata olives, pitted and sliced
- 2 tablespoons olive oil
- 3 tablespoons lemon juice
- Salt and pepper to taste

Direction

1. Prep air fryer to 400 degrees F for 5 minutes.
2. Brush steaks with oil.
3. Season with salt and pepper.
4. Add to the air fryer oven.
5. Choose air fry option.
6. Cook the steaks for 5 to 6 minutes per side.
7. Mix the tapenade ingredients.
8. Serve steak with tapenade.

Nutrition: Calories: 277 Fat: 14g Proteins: 23g.

Steak Salad

Preparation Time: 31 minutes
Cooking Time: 60 minutes
Serving: 4
Ingredients:
Steak

- 2 rib eye steaks, sliced into strips
- 2 teaspoons garlic, minced
- 1/4 cup soy sauce
- 1/4 cup honey
- 1/4 cup bourbon
- 1/4 cup Worcestershire sauce
- 1/4 cup brown sugar
- 1/2 teaspoon red pepper flakes

Salad

- 4 cups Romaine lettuce
- 1/4 cup red onions, sliced
- 1/2 cucumber, diced
- 1 cup cherry tomatoes, sliced in half
- 1/2 mozzarella cheese, shredded

Directions
1. Add the steaks to a bowl.
2. In another bowl, mix the steak ingredients.
3. Pour mixture into the steak strips.
4. Chill to marinate for 1 hour.
5. Prep your air fryer at 400 degrees F for 5 minutes.
6. Select air fry option.
7. Cook the steak strips for 5 minutes per side.
8. Toss the salad ingredients in a large bowl.
9. Top with the steak strips.

Nutrition: Calories: 281 Fat: 19g Proteins: 31g.

Meatballs

Preparation Time: 9 minutes
Cooking Time: 8 minutes
Serving: 4

Ingredients:

- 1/2 lb. ground beef
- 1/2 cup ground pork
- 1 onion, chopped
- 2 cloves garlic, minced
- 2 teaspoons dried basil
- 2 teaspoons dried oregano
- 2 teaspoons dried parsley
- 1 cup breadcrumbs
- 1 egg, beaten
- 1/2 cup Parmesan cheese
- Salt and pepper to taste
- Cooking spray

Directions

1. Combine all the ingredients
2. Mix well.
3. Form balls from the mixture.
4. Spray with oil.
5. Add the meatballs to the air fryer oven.
6. Choose air fry option.
7. Cook at 350 degrees F for 4 minutes per side.

Nutrition: Calories: 251 Fat: 15g Proteins: 28g.

Beef Enchilada

Preparation Time: 4 minutes
Cooking Time: 16 minutes
Serving: 2

Ingredients:

- 1 cup lean ground beef, cooked
- 2 teaspoons taco seasoning
- 1/4 cup tomatoes, chopped
- 1/4 cup black beans
- 1/4 cup enchilada sauce
- 2 tortillas

Directions

1. Season the ground beef with taco seasoning.
2. Mix with the tomatoes and black beans.
3. Top the tortillas with the beef mixture.
4. Sprinkle cheese on top.
5. Roll up the tortillas.
6. Place in the air fryer.
7. Brush with the enchilada sauce.
8. Select air fry setting.
9. Cook at 350F for 10 minutes both sides.

Nutrition: Calories: 281 Fat: 15g Proteins: 22g.

Seafood recipes

Cilantro-Lime Fried Shrimp

Preparation Time: 10 minutes
Cooking Time: 9 minutes
Servings: 4

Ingredients:

- pound raw shrimp, peeled and deveined with tails on or off (see Prep tip)
- ½ cup chopped fresh cilantro
- Juice of 1 lime
- 1 egg
- ½ cup all-purpose flour
- ¾ cup bread crumbs
- Salt
- Pepper
- Cooking oil
- ½ cup cocktail sauce (optional)

Directions:

1. Preparing the Ingredients. Place the shrimp in a plastic bag and add the cilantro and lime juice. Seal the bag. Shake to combine. Marinate in the refrigerator for 30 minutes.
2. In a small bowl, beat the egg. In another small bowl, place the flour. Place the bread crumbs in a third small bowl, and season with salt and pepper to taste.
3. Spray the air fryer rack/basket with cooking oil.

4. Remove the shrimp from the plastic bag. Dip each in the flour, then the egg, and then the bread crumbs.
5. Air Frying. Place the shrimp in the XL air fryer oven. It is okay to stack them. Spray the shrimp with cooking oil. Cook for 4 minutes.
6. Open the air fryer oven and flip the shrimp. I recommend flipping individually instead of shaking to keep the breading intact. Cook for an additional 4 minutes, or until crisp.
7. Cool before serving. Serve with cocktail sauce if desired.

Nutrition: Calories: 254 Fat: 4g Protein: 29g

Lemony Tuna

Preparation Time: 10 minutes
Cooking Time: 9 minutes
Servings: 4
Ingredients:

- 2 (6-ounce) cans water packed plain tuna
- 2 teaspoons Dijon mustard
- ½ cup breadcrumbs
- tablespoon fresh lime juice
- tablespoons fresh parsley, chopped
- 1 egg
- Chef man of hot sauce
- tablespoons canola oil
- Salt and freshly ground black pepper, to taste

Directions:

1. Preparing the Ingredients. Drain most of the liquid from the canned tuna.

2. In a bowl, add the fish, mustard, crumbs, citrus juice, parsley, and hot sauce and mix till well combined. Add a little canola oil if it seems too dry. Add egg, salt and stir to combine. Make the patties from tuna mixture. Refrigerate the tuna patties for about 2 hours.

3. Air Frying. Preheat the air fryer oven to 355 degrees F. Cook for about 10-12 minutes.

Nutrition: Calories 599 Fat 37g Protein 55g

Grilled Soy Salmon Fillets

Preparation Time: 5 minutes
Cooking Time: 8 minutes
Servings: 4

Ingredients:

- 4 salmon fillets
- 1/4 teaspoon ground black pepper
- 1/2 teaspoon cayenne pepper
- 1/2 teaspoon salt
- teaspoon onion powder
- 1 tablespoon fresh lemon juice
- 1/2 cup soy sauce
- 1/2 cup water
- 1 tablespoon honey
- tablespoons extra-virgin olive oil

Directions:

1. Preparing the Ingredients. Firstly, pat the salmon fillets dry using kitchen towels. Season the salmon with black pepper, cayenne pepper, salt, and onion powder.
2. To make the marinade, combine together the lemon juice, soy sauce, water, honey, and olive oil. Marinate the salmon for at least 2 hours in your refrigerator.
3. Arrange the fish fillets on a grill basket in your XL air fryer oven.
4. Air Frying. Bake at 330 degrees for 8 to 9 minutes, or until salmon fillets are easily flaked with a fork.

5. Work with batches and serve warm.

Nutrition: Calories 814 Fat 39g Protein 70g

Old Bay Crab Cakes

Preparation Time: 10 minutes
Cooking Time: 19 minutes
Servings: 4

Ingredients:

- 2 slices dried bread, crusts removed
- Small amount of milk
- tablespoon mayonnaise
- 1 tablespoon Worcestershire sauce
- 1 tablespoon baking powder
- 1 tablespoon parsley flakes
- 1 teaspoon Old Bay® Seasoning
- 1/4 teaspoon salt
- 1 egg
- 1-pound lump crabmeat

Directions:

1. Preparing the Ingredients. Crush your bread over a large bowl until it is broken down into small pieces. Add milk and stir until bread crumbs are moistened. Mix in mayo and Worcestershire sauce. Add remaining ingredients and mix well. Shape into 4 patties.

2. Air Frying. Cook at 360 degrees for 20 minutes, flip half way through.

Nutrition: Calories: 165 Fat: 4.5g Protein: 24g

Scallops and Spring Veggies

Preparation Time: 10 minutes
Cooking Time: 9 minutes   Servings: 4
Ingredients:

- ½ pound asparagus ends trimmed, cut into 2-inch pieces
- cup sugars snap peas
- 1-pound sea scallops
- 1 tablespoon lemon juice
- teaspoons olive oil
- ½ teaspoon dried thyme
- Pinch salt
- Freshly ground black pepper

Directions:

1. Preparing the Ingredients. Place the asparagus and sugar snap peas in the Oven rack/basket. Place the Rack on the middle-shelf of the XL air fryer oven.

2. Air Frying. Cook for 2 to 3 minutes or until the vegetables are just starting to get tender.

3. Meanwhile, check the scallops for a small muscle attached to the side, and pull it off and discard.

4. In a medium bowl, toss the scallops with the lemon juice, olive oil, thyme, salt, and pepper. Place into the Oven rack/basket on top of the vegetables. Place the Rack on the middle-shelf of the XL air fryer oven.

5. Air Frying. Steam for 5 to 7 minutes. Until the scallops are just firm, and the vegetables are tender. Serve immediately.

Nutrition: Calories: 162 Fat: 4g Protein: 22g

Fried Calamari

Preparation Time: 8 minutes
Cooking Time: 7 minutes
Servings: 6

Ingredients:

- ½ tsp. salt
- ½ tsp. Old Bay seasoning
- 1/3 C. plain cornmeal
- ½ C. semolina flour
- ½ C. almond flour
- 5-6 C. olive oil
- ½ pounds baby squid

Directions:

1. Preparing the Ingredients. Rinse squid in cold water and slice tentacles, keeping just ¼-inch of the hood in one piece.
2. Combine 1-2 pinches of pepper, salt, Old Bay seasoning, cornmeal, and both flours together. Dredge squid pieces into flour mixture and place into the XL air fryer oven.
3. Air Frying. Spray liberally with olive oil. Cook 15 minutes at 345 degrees till coating turns a golden brown.

Nutrition: Calories: 211 Fat: 6g Protein: 21g

Vegetable

and side recipes

Tomato Green Bean Soup

Preparation Time: 10 minutes
Cooking Time: 6 hours
Serving: 8

Ingredients:

- 1 lb. fresh green beans cut into 1-inch pieces
- 1 cup carrots, chopped
- 3 cups fresh tomatoes, diced
- 1 garlic clove, minced
- 6 cups vegetable broth
- 1/4 tsp black pepper
- 1 cup onions, chopped
- 1 tsp basil, dried
- 1/2 tsp salt

Directions:

1. Place the inner pot in the grill air fryer combo base.
2. Add all ingredients into the inner pot and stir well.
3. Cover the inner pot with a glass lid.
4. Select slow cook mode then press the temperature button and set the time for 6 hours. Click start.
5. When the timer reaches 0, then press the cancel button.
6. Serve and enjoy.

Nutrition: Calories 71 Fat 1.3g Protein 5.6g

Curried Tomato Soup

Preparation Time: 10 minutes
Cooking Time: 6 hours
Serving: 8
Ingredients
:

- 4 lb. tomatoes, cored and diced
- 2 tbsp. onion, minced
- 1 tsp garlic, minced
- 2 tsp curry powder
- 2 cups of coconut milk
- 1 cup of water
- 1 tsp salt

Directions:

1. Place the inner pot in the grill air fryer combo base.
2. Add all ingredients into the inner pot and stir well.
3. Cover the inner pot with a glass lid.
4. Select slow cook mode then press the temperature button and set the time for 6 hours. Click start.
5. When the timer reaches 0, then press the cancel button.
6. Puree the soup using a blender until smooth.
7. Stir well and serve.

Nutrition: Calories 182 Fat 14.8g Protein 3.5g

Stuffed Pepper

Preparation Time: 10 minutes
Cooking Time: 25 minutes
Serving: 4

Ingredients:

- 4 eggs
- 1/4 cup baby broccoli florets
- 1/4 cup cherry tomatoes
- 1 tsp dried sage
- 2.5 oz. cheddar cheese, grated
- 7 oz. almond milk
- 2 bell peppers, cut in half and deseeded
- Pepper
- Salt

Directions:

1. In a bowl, whisk together eggs, milk, broccoli, cherry tomatoes, sage, pepper, and salt.
2. Pour egg mixture into the bell pepper halves.
3. Sprinkle cheese on top of bell pepper.
4. Place the inner pot in the grill air fryer combo base.
5. Place stuffed peppers into the inner pot.
6. Cover the inner pot with an air frying lid.
7. Select bake mode then set the temperature to 390 F and time for 25 minutes. Click start.
8. When the timer reaches 0, then press the cancel button.
9. Serve and enjoy.

Nutrition: Calories 285 Fat 25.2g Protein 11.5g

Healthy Artichoke Casserole

Preparation Time: 10 minutes
Cooking Time: 30 minutes
Serving: 12

Ingredients:

- 16 eggs
- 14 oz. can artichoke hearts, drained and cut into pieces
- 1/4 cup coconut milk
- 1/2 tsp red pepper, crushed
- 1/2 tsp thyme, diced
- 1/2 cup ricotta cheese
- 1/2 cup parmesan cheese
- 1 cup cheddar cheese, shredded
- 10 oz. frozen spinach, thawed and drain well
- 1 garlic clove, minced
- 1/4 cup onion, shaved
- 1 tsp salt

Directions:

1. In a large bowl, whisk together eggs and coconut milk.
2. Add spinach and artichoke into the egg mixture.
3. Add all remaining ingredients except ricotta cheese and stir well to combine.
4. Place the inner pot in the grill air fryer combo base.
5. Pour egg mixture into the inner pot.

6. Spread ricotta cheese on top of the egg mixture.

7. Cover the inner pot with an air frying lid.

8. Select bake mode then set the temperature to 350 F and time for 30 minutes. Click start.

9. When the timer reaches 0, then press the cancel button.

10. Serve and enjoy.

Nutrition: Calories 205 Fat 13.7g Protein 15.9g

Golden Eggplant Slices with Parsley

Preparation Time: 5 minutes
Cooking Time: 12 minutes
Servings: 4

Ingredients:

- cup flour
- 4 eggs
- Salt, to taste
- cups bread crumbs
- 1 teaspoon Italian seasoning
- eggplants, sliced
- 2 garlic cloves, sliced
- 2 tablespoons chopped parsley
- Cooking spray

Direction

1. Spritz the air fry basket with cooking spray. Set aside.
2. On a plate, place the flour. In a shallow bowl, whisk the eggs with salt. In another shallow bowl, combine the bread crumbs and Italian seasoning.
3. Dredge the eggplant slices, one at a time, in the flour, then in the whisked eggs, finally in the bread crumb mixture to coat well.

4. Lay the coated eggplant slices in the air fry basket.
5. Place the basket on the air fry position.
6. Select Air Fry, set temperature to 390°F (199°C), and set time to 12 minutes. Flip the eggplant slices halfway through the cooking time.
7. When cooking is complete, the eggplant slices should be golden brown and crispy. Transfer the eggplant slices to a plate and sprinkle the parsley and garlic on top before serving.

Nutrition: Calories 874 Fat 37g Protein 79g

Toasted-Baked Tofu Cubes

Preparation Time: 15 minutes
Cooking Time: 17 minutes
Servings: 2

Ingredients:

- 1/2 block of tofu, cubed
- tbsp. olive oil
- 1 tbsp. nutritional yeast
- 1 tbsp. flour
- 1/4 tsp. black pepper
- 1 tsp. sea salt
- 1/2 tsp. garlic powder

Directions

1. Combine all the ingredients with tofu
2. Preheat the Air Fryer Grill at 2300C or 4000F.
3. Bake tofu on a lined baking tray for 15-30 minutes; turn it around every 10 minutes.

Nutrition: Calories: 100 Protein: 8g Fat 6g

Veggie Rolls

Preparation Time: 20 minutes
Cooking Time: 20 minutes Servings: 5
Ingredients:

- 1 tablespoon olive oil
- 1 clove garlic, minced
- 1 teaspoon ginger, minced
- 3 scallions, chopped
- ½ lb. mushrooms, chopped
- 2 cups cabbage, chopped
- 8 oz. water chestnuts, diced
- Salt and pepper to taste
- 6 spring roll wrappers
- 1 tablespoon water

Direction

1. Add oil to a pan over medium heat.
2. Cook the garlic, ginger, scallions and mushrooms for 2 minutes.
3. Stir in the remaining vegetables.
4. Season with salt and pepper.
5. Cook for 3 minutes, stirring. Transfer to a strainer.
6. Add vegetables on top of the wrappers.
7. Roll up the wrappers.
8. Seal the edges with water.
9. Place the rolls inside the air fryer.
10. Choose air fry setting.
11. Cook at 360 degrees F for 15 minutes.

Nutrition: Calories 805 Fat 33g Protein 92g

Toasted Vegetables with Rice and Eggs

Preparation Time: 5 minutes
Cooking Time: 13 minutes   Servings: 4
Ingredients:

- 2 teaspoons melted butter
- cup chopped mushrooms
- 1 cup cooked rice
- 1 cup peas
- 1 carrot, chopped
- 1 red onion, chopped
- 1 garlic clove, minced
- Salt and black pepper, to taste
- hard-boiled eggs, grated
- 1 tablespoon soy sauce

Direction

Coat a baking dish with melted butter. Stir together the mushrooms, carrot, peas, garlic, onion, cooked rice, salt, and pepper in a large bowl until well mixed. Pour the mixture into the prepared baking dish. Place the baking dish on the toast position. Select Toast, set temperature to 380°F (193°C), and set time to 12 minutes.

When cooking is complete, remove from the air fryer grill. Divide the mixture among four plates. Serve warm with a sprinkle of grated eggs and a drizzle of soy sauce.

Nutrition: Calories 724 Fat 37g Protein 62g

Dessert

Chocolate Donuts

Preparation Time: 15 minutes
Cooking Time: 16 minutes
Servings: 10

Ingredients:

- 8-ounce jumbo biscuits
- Cooking oil
- Chocolate sauce, such as Hershey's

Directions:

1. Separate the biscuit dough into 8 biscuits and place them on a flat work surface. Cut a hole in the center of each biscuit using a small circle cookie cutter. You can also cut the holes using a knife.
2. Spray the air fryer basket with cooking oil. Place 4 donuts in the air fryer. Do not stack. Spray with cooking oil. Air fry for 4 minutes.
3. Flip the donuts, then air fry for an additional 4 minutes. Remove the cooked donuts from the air fryer, repeat steps 3 and 4 for the remaining 4 donuts. Drizzle chocolate sauce over the donuts and enjoy while warm.

Nutrition: Calories: 240 Fat: 14g Protein: 3g

Fried Bananas with Chocolate Sauce

Preparation Time: 15 minutes
Cooking Time: 11 minutes
Servings: 2

Ingredients:

- large egg
- ¼ cup cornstarch
- ¼ cup plain bread crumbs
- bananas, halved crosswise
- Cooking oil
- Chocolate sauce

Directions:

1. In a small bowl, beat the egg. In another bowl, place the cornstarch. Put the bread crumbs in your third bowl. Dip the bananas in the cornstarch, then the egg, and then the bread crumbs.
2. Spray the air fryer basket with cooking oil. Place the bananas in the basket and spray them with cooking oil.
3. Air fry for 5 minutes. Open the air fryer and flip the bananas. Cook for an additional 2 minutes. Transfer the bananas to plates. Put the chocolate sauce on the bananas, and serve.

Nutrition: Calories: 130 Fat: 6g Protein: 2g

Apple Hand Pies

Preparation Time: 15 minutes
Cooking Time: 8 minutes
Servings: 6

Ingredients:

- 15-ounces no-sugar-added apple pie filling
- store-bought crust

Directions:

1. Layout pie crust and slice into equal-sized squares. Place 2 tbsp. filling into each square and seal the crust with a fork. Place into the air fryer. Bake for 8 minutes at 390 F until golden in color.

Nutrition: Calories: 135 Fat: 6g Protein: 1g

Sweet Cream Cheese Wontons

Preparation Time: 15 minutes
Cooking Time: 5 minutes
Servings: 16

Ingredients:

- egg mixed with a bit of water
- Wonton wrappers
- ½ cup powdered sweetener
- 8 ounces softened cream cheese
- Olive oil

Directions:

1. Mix sweetener and cream cheese together. Layout 4 wontons at a time and cover with a dish towel to prevent drying out. Place ½ of a teaspoon of cream cheese mixture into each wrapper.
2. Dip finger into egg/water mixture and fold diagonally to form a triangle. Seal edges well. Repeat with the remaining ingredients.
3. Place filled wontons into the air fryer and air fry for 5 minutes at 400 degrees, shaking halfway through cooking.

Nutrition: Calories: 250 Fat: 13g Protein: 6g

Keto Chaffle

Egg and Cheddar Cheese Chaffle

Preparation time: 10 minutes
Cooking Time: 7-9 Minutes
Servings: 4
Ingredients:
Batter

- 4 eggs
- 2 cups shredded white cheddar cheese
- Salt and pepper to taste

Other

- 2 tablespoons butter for brushing the waffle maker
- 4 large eggs
- 2 tablespoons olive oil

Directions:
1. Preheat the waffle maker.
2. Beat the eggs into a bowl and whisk them with a fork.
3. Stir in the grated cheddar cheese and season with salt and pepper. Brush the heated waffle maker with butter and add a few tablespoons of the batter.
4. Close the lid and Cooking for about 7–8 minutes depending on your waffle maker.
5. While chaffles are Cooking, Cooking the eggs.
6. Set the oil in a large non-stick pan that has a lid over medium-low heat for 2-3 minutes
7. Crack an egg in a small ramekin and gently add it to the pan. Repeat the same way for the other 3 eggs.
8. Cover and let Cooking for 2 to 2 1/2 minutes for set eggs but with runny yolks. Remove from heat.
9. To serve, place a chaffle on each plate and top with an egg. Flavor with salt and black pepper to taste.

Nutrition: Calories: 74 Total Fat: 7g Carbs: 1g Net Carbs: 0g Fiber: 0g Protein: 3g

Chili Chaffle

Preparation time: 10 minutes
Cooking Time: 7-9 Minutes
Servings: 4
Ingredients:
Batter

- 4 eggs
- 1/2 cup grated parmesan cheese
- 11/2 cups grated yellow cheddar cheese
- 1 hot red chili pepper
- Salt and pepper to taste
- 1/2 teaspoon dried garlic powder
- 1 teaspoon dried basil
- 2 tablespoons almond flour

Other

- 2 tablespoons olive oil for brushing the waffle maker

Directions:
1. Preheat the waffle maker.
2. Whisk the eggs into a bowl and add the grated parmesan and cheddar cheese.
3. Mix until just combined and add the chopped chili pepper. Season with salt and pepper, dried garlic powder and dried basil. Stir in the almond flour.
4. Mix until everything is combined.
5. Brush the heated waffle maker with olive oil and add a few tablespoons of the batter.
6. Close the lid and Cooking for about 7–8 minutes depending on your waffle maker.

Nutrition: Calories: 859 Total Fat: 73g Carbs: 8g Net Carbs: 8g Fiber: 0g Protein: 41g

Simple Savory Chaffle

Preparation time: 10 minutes
Cooking Time: 7–9 Minutes
Servings: 4
Ingredients:
Batter

- 4 eggs
- 1 cup grated Mozzarella cheese
- 1 cup grated provolone cheese
- 1/2 cup almond flour
- 2 tablespoons coconut flour
- 21/2 teaspoons baking powder
- Salt and pepper to taste

Other

- 2 tablespoons butter to brush the waffle maker

Directions:

1. Preheat the waffle maker.
2. Add the grated Mozzarella and provolone cheese to a bowl and mix.
3. Add the almond and coconut flour and baking powder and season with salt and pepper.
4. Mix with a wire whisk and crack in the eggs.
5. Stir everything together until batter forms.
6. Brush the heated waffle maker with butter and add a few tablespoons of the batter.
7. Close the lid and Cooking for about 8 minutes depending on your waffle maker.
8. Serve and enjoy.

Nutrition: Calories: 248 Total Fat: 18g Carbs: 11g Net Carbs: 7g Fiber: 5g Protein: 14g

Pumpkin Chaffle with Cream Cheese Frosting

Preparation Time: 3 minutes
Cooking Time: 8 minutes
Servings: 2

Ingredients:

- 1 egg
- 1/2 cup of mozzarella cheese
- 1/2 tsp. pumpkin pie spice
- 1 tbs. pumpkin solid packed with no sugar added
- Optional Cream Cheese Frosting Ingredients:
- 2 tbs. softened and room temperature cream cheese
- 2 tbs. any of your favorite keto-friendly sweetener
- 1/2 tsp. clear extract of vanilla

Directions:

1. Heat the mini waffle maker.
2. Whip the egg in a little bowl.
3. Mix the cheese, pumpkin pie spice, and pumpkin in a mixing bowl.
4. Mix well.
5. Cooking for at least 3 to 4 minutes, until golden brown, in the mini waffle maker with half of the mixture.
6. When the chaffle is baking, mix all of the ingredients for the cream cheese frosting in a mixing bowl and whisk until smooth and fluffy.
7. Serve the hot chaffle with the cream cheese frosting right away.

Nutrition: Calories: 266 Carbohydrates: 2g Fat: 23g Protein: 13g

Chaffle Bread Pudding With Cranberries

Preparation Time: 10 minutes
Cooking Time: 30 minutes
Servings: 2
Ingredients:
Chaffles:

- 4 eggs
- 1 cup of shredded part skim mozzarella - cheese

Pudding:

- 3 beaten eggs
- 2 tsp. extract of vanilla
- 2 tsp. pumpkin pie spice
- 1/4 cup of So Nourished Erythritol sweetener blend
- 1/2 cup of canned pumpkin
- 1/2 cup of heavy cream
- 1/2 cup of fresh or frozen cranberries
- 1 tbsp. granulated Erythritol to sprinkle on top

Directions:
Chaffles:

1. Heat the waffle maker
2. In a mixing bowl, merge together the eggs and grated cheese.
3. Cooking chaffles in a waffle maker; depending on the unit, you'll get 4-6 chaffles/waffles.
4. Cooking 1/4 cup of batter at a time in a mini waffle machine (3-4 minutes every)
5. You can cook all of the batter at once in a full-size waffle maker for around 7 minutes.
6. Allow chaffles to cool on a rack before serving.

Bread Pudding:
1. Heat the oven to 350F. Tear the chaffles into bite-size bits with your hands.
2. Mix beaten eggs, milk, pumpkin, vanilla, spice blend, and sweetener in a mixing bowl.
3. To mix, whisk all together thoroughly.
4. Pour onto a pie plate that has been greased.
5. Top with cranberries and a little sugar if needed (if desired)
6. Heat oven to 350F and bake for 30 minutes, or until set.
7. Serve warm or cold with ice cream on top (if desired)

Nutrition: Calories: 160 Total Fat: 12g Cholesterol: 24mg Sodium: 93mg Carbohydrates: 4g Fiber: 1g
Sugar: 1g Protein: 9g

Chaffles with Zucchini Topping

Preparation Time: 10 minutes
Cooking Time: 10 minutes
Servings: 2

Ingredients:
- 1 large egg
- 1 tbsp. almond flour
- 1 tbsp. full-fat Greek yogurt
- 1/8 tsp. baking powder
- 1/4 cup shredded Swiss cheese

Topping:
- 4oz. grill prawns
- 4 oz. steamed cauliflower mash
- 1/2 zucchini sliced
- 3 lettuce leaves
- 1 tomato, sliced
- 1 tbsp. flax seeds

Directions:
1. Make 3 chaffles with the given chaffles ingredients.
2. For serving, arrange lettuce leaves on each chaffle.
3. Top with zucchini slice, grill prawns, cauliflower mash and a tomato slice.
4. Drizzle flax seeds on top.
5. Serve and enjoy!

Nutrition: Protein: 45 Fat: 47 Carbohydrates: 8

Chaffle with Melted Cheese and Bacon

Preparation Time: 10 minutes
Cooking Time: 15 minutes
Servings: 2

Ingredients:

- 1 egg
- 1/2 cup cheddar cheese, shredded
- 1 tbsp. parmesan cheese
- 3/4 tsp. coconut flour
- 1/4 tsp. baking powder
- 1/8 tsp. Italian Seasoning
- Pinch of salt
- 1/4 tsp. garlic powder

For Topping:

- 1 bacon sliced, Cooked and chopped
- 1/2 cup mozzarella cheese, shredded
- 1/4 tsp. parsley, chopped

Directions:

1. Preheat oven to 400 degrees.
2. Switch on your Mini Waffle Maker and grease with Cooking spray.
3. Mix together chaffle ingredients in a mixing bowl until combined.

4. Spoon half of the batter in the center of the waffle maker and close the lid. Cooking chaffles for about 3 minutes until cooked.
5. Carefully remove chaffles from the maker.
6. Arrange chaffles in a greased baking tray.
7. Top with mozzarella cheese, chopped bacon and parsley.
8. And bake in the oven for 4-5 minutes.
9. Once the cheese is melted, remove from the oven.
10. Serve and enjoy!

Nutrition: Protein: 28 Fat: 69 Carbohydrates: 3

Pumpkin Chaffles

Preparation Time: 5 minutes
Cooking Time: 8 minutes
Servings: 2

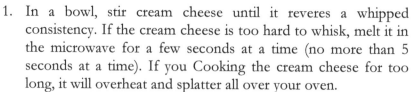

Ingredients:

- 1 oz. softened cream cheese
- 1 large egg
- 1 tbsp. pumpkin puree
- 1/2 tsp. pumpkin spice
- 1 tbsp. superfine almond flour
- 1/4 tsp. baking powder
- 1/2 tsp. Erythritol granular

Directions:

1. In a bowl, stir cream cheese until it reveres a whipped consistency. If the cream cheese is too hard to whisk, melt it in the microwave for a few seconds at a time (no more than 5 seconds at a time). If you Cooking the cream cheese for too long, it will overheat and splatter all over your oven.
2. In another bowl, merge together the egg and pumpkin puree until creamy. Whisk in the pumpkin spice and almond flour until well mixed. Whether you're using baking powder and sweetener, mix them together so they're equally distributed.
3. Waffle iron should be preheated. Grease the waffle iron with Cooking oil spray when it's ready.
4. Half of the batter can be poured into the mini waffle maker. Your batter should fill in all of the gaps. Waffle iron should be closed. Allow for 4-5 minutes of Cooking time, or until the waffle is dark brown and crispy on the outside. Continue for the remaining hitter. Using the Dash mini waffle machine, you should have enough batter to produce two chaffles.

Nutrition: Calories: 116.26 Carbohydrates: 2.61g Protein: 4.52g Fat: 9.54g Cholesterol: 121.1mg Potassium: 131.34mg,

Spicy Shrimp and Chaffles

Preparation time: 9 minutes
Cooking Time: 31 Minutes
Servings: 4

Ingredients:

For the shrimp:
- 1 tbsp. olive oil
- 1 lb. jumbo shrimp, peeled and deveined
- 1 tbsp. Creole seasoning
- Salt to taste
- 2 tbsp. hot sauce
- 3 tbsp. butter
- 2 tbsp. chopped fresh scallions to garnish

For the chaffles:
- 2 eggs, beaten
- 1 cup finely grated Monterey Jack cheese

Directions:

For the shrimp:
1. Set the olive oil in a medium skillet over medium heat.
2. Season the shrimp with the Creole seasoning and salt. Cooking in the oil until pink and opaque on both sides, 2 minutes.
3. Pour in the hot sauce and butter. Mix well until the shrimp is adequately coated in the sauce, 1 minute.
4. Turn the heat off and set aside.

For the chaffles:

1. Preheat the waffle iron.
2. In a medium bowl, merge the eggs and Monterey Jack cheese.
3. Open the iron and add a quarter of the mixture. Close and Cooking until crispy, 7 minutes.
4. Transfer the chaffle to a plate and make 3 more chaffles in the same manner.
5. Cut the chaffles into quarters and place on a plate.
6. Set with the shrimp and garnish with the scallions.
7. Serve warm.

Nutrition: Calories 342 Fats 19.75g Carbs 2.8g Net Carbs 2.3g Protein 36.01g

Creamy Chicken Chaffle Sandwich

Preparation time: 10 minutes
Cooking Time: 10 Minutes
Servings: 2

Ingredients:

- Cooking spray
- 1 cup chicken breast fillet, cubed
- Salt and pepper to taste
- 1/4 cup all-purpose cream
- 4 garlic chaffles
- Parsley, chopped

Directions:

1. Spray your pan with oil.
2. Put it over medium heat.
3. Add the chicken fillet cubes.
4. Season with salt and pepper.
5. Reduce heat and add the cream.
6. Spread chicken mixture on top of the chaffle.
7. Garnish with parsley and top with another chaffle.

Nutrition: Calories 273 Total Fat 34g Saturated Fat 4.1g Cholesterol 62mg Sodium 373mg Total Carbohydrate 22.5g Protein 17.5g Potassium 177mg

Chaffle Cannoli

Preparation time: 9 minutes
Cooking Time: 28 Minutes
Servings: 2
Ingredients:
For the chaffles:

- 1 large egg
- 1 egg yolk
- 3 tbsp. butter, melted
- 1 tbsp. swerve confectioner's
- 1 cup finely grated Parmesan cheese
- 2 tbsp. finely grated mozzarella cheese

For the cannoli filling:

- 1/2 cup ricotta cheese
- 2 tbsp. swerve confectioner's sugar
- 1 tsp. vanilla extract
- 2 tbsp. unsweetened chocolate chips for garnishing

Directions:

1. Preheat the waffle iron. Meanwhile, in a medium bowl, merge all the ingredients for the chaffles.
2. Open the iron; pour in a quarter of the mixture, cover, and Cooking until crispy, 7 minutes.
3. Remove the chaffle onto a plate and make 3 more with the remaining batter.
4. Meanwhile, for the cannoli filling:
5. Beat the ricotta cheese and swerve confectioner's sugar until smooth. Mix in the vanilla.
6. On each chaffle, spread some of the filling and wrap over.
7. Garnish the creamy ends with some chocolate chips.
8. Serve immediately.

Nutrition: Calories 308 Fats 25.05g Carbs 5.17g Net Carbs 5.17g Protein 15.18g

Strawberry Shortcake Chaffle Bowls

Preparation time: 15 minutes
Cooking Time: 28 Minutes
Servings: 2

Ingredients:

- 1 egg, beaten
- 1/2 cup finely grated mozzarella cheese
- 1 tbsp. almond flour
- 1/4 tsp. baking powder
- 2 drops cake batter extract
- 1 cup cream cheese, softened
- 1 cup fresh strawberries, sliced
- 1 tbsp. sugar-free maple syrup

Directions:

1. Preheat a waffle bowl maker and grease lightly with Cooking spray.
2. Meanwhile, in a medium bowl, whisk all the ingredients except the cream cheese and strawberries.
3. Open the iron; pour in half of the mixture, cover, and Cooking until crispy, 6 to 7 minutes.
4. Remove the chaffle bowl onto a plate and set aside.
5. Make a second chaffle bowl with the remaining batter.
6. To serve, divide the cream cheese into the chaffle bowls and top with the strawberries.
7. Drizzle the filling with the maple syrup and serve.

Nutrition: Calories 235 Fats 20.62g Carbs 5.9g Net Carbs 5g Protein 7.51g

Thank You!

Lightning Source UK Ltd.
Milton Keynes UK
UKHW021123180621
385684UK00001B/5